SEV
WONDERS
of the ANCIENT WORLD

ARIANNE McHUGH

red rhino
b∞ks®
NONFICTION

Area 51

Cloning

Drones

Fault Lines

Great Spies of the World

Monsters of the Deep

Monsters on Land

Seven Wonders of the Ancient World

Virtual Reality

Witchcraft

Wormholes

Photo credits: page 32: Alamy.com; All other source images from Shutterstock.com

SADDLEBACK
EDUCATIONAL PUBLISHING
www.sdlback.com

ISBN-13: 978-1-68021-035-4
ISBN-10: 1-68021-035-1
eBook: 978-1-63078-342-6

Printed in Malaysia

20 19 18 17 16   2 3 4 5

TABLE OF CONTENTS

A CLOSER LOOK

Chapter 1

INCREDIBLE SIGHTS

You are in Iraq.

The desert is vast.

It goes for miles.

Then you see a green mound.

You take a closer look.

Can it be?

It is.

A mountain of plants.

But this is no normal mountain.

It is a garden.
And it is beautiful.
Flowers and vines 75 feet up.
Blue, red, yellow, pink blooms.
Green everywhere.

It seems impossible.
This is the desert.
How could gardens be here?

A different place.

Egypt.

Three *pyramids*.

Too perfect not to notice.

Too tall to ignore.

Majestic.

Where did they come from?
What is inside?
You move closer.
You stand in awe.
You want to take pictures.
Share them with everyone.
You are not alone.

Over 2,000 years ago
these places existed.
Or did they?
Some may be myths.
We know one is real.
It remains today.

Travelers talked about these places.
They called them wonders.
Seven in all.
Incredible sights to be seen.

Chapter 2

ANCIENT STORYTELLING

Ancient history.

The beginning of time.

Thousands of years ago.

Before cameras.

Before there was paper.

What was it like?

People study the past.
They look at *artifacts*.
These are objects.
Found in the ground.
Data is collected.
It is studied.
We know when people lived.
And died.
When wars started.
And ended.
History comes to life.
A story is told.

The seven wonders are very old.

Ancient.

Most are no longer here.

They are part of the past.

How do we know about them?

From stories.

Ones told long ago.

Imagine.

A time with no TV.

No Internet. No phones.

People would talk. Tell stories.

Entertain. Inform.

Great storytellers drew crowds.

People listened.

They believed.

13

Stories would travel.

The best would go far.

Stories would have to be grand.

They would have to be rare.

That's how they would last.

And be told for years to come.

The wonders were great stories.

Perhaps the greatest.

People would hear them.

And travel for miles.

Were the stories real?

They wanted to see with their eyes.

They wanted to know the truth.

The truth of the wonders.

15

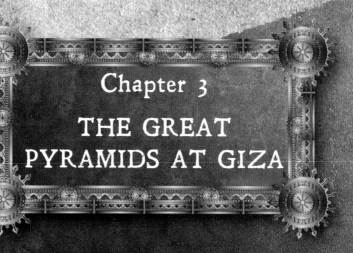

Chapter 3

THE GREAT PYRAMIDS AT GIZA

This story took place in Egypt.

Three huge pyramids.

They rose from the desert.

One was the largest.

482 feet tall.

Made of polished *limestone*.

It glowed white.

On top, a gold cap sparkled.

It covered 13 acres.

THE GREAT PYRAMIDS AT GIZA

Date built: 2560–2680 BC
Location: Egypt
How long to build: 20 years
What happened: Nothing. Still exists today.

But what was inside?

Each was said to be a tomb.

A place a *pharaoh* was buried.

One king for each pyramid.

The largest was for King Khufu.

Some of his treasure was buried too.

The inside was like a maze.

There were secret rooms.

Huge stones blocked some halls.

This kept robbers out.

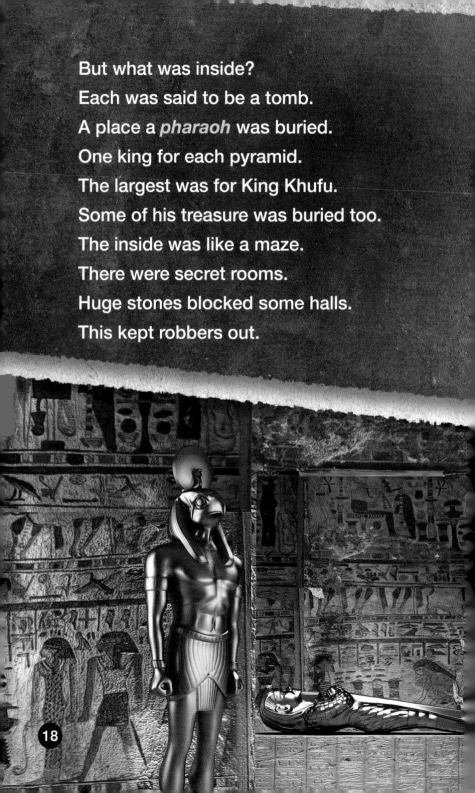

How were they built?

There were no cranes.

No trucks.

They used slaves.

The slaves moved the stones.

They used ramps.

And ropes.

The blocks were moved on logs.

Is this why it took so long?

It took 20 years to build.

This is the only wonder still standing today.

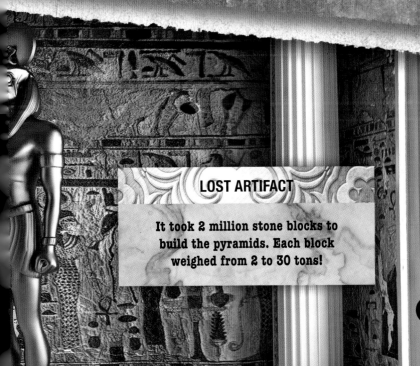

LOST ARTIFACT

It took 2 million stone blocks to build the pyramids. Each block weighed from 2 to 30 tons!

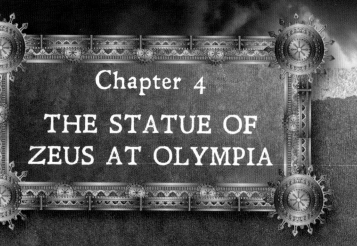

Chapter 4

THE STATUE OF ZEUS AT OLYMPIA

Zeus was a Greek god.

The god of thunder.

And the king of all gods.

A *temple* was built.

To honor Zeus.

It was a place to store gifts.

Items to *adorn* him.

Show his worth.

Inside the temple was the *statue*.

It was 40 feet tall.

The statue was of Zeus.

He sat on a large throne.

People would say, "Imagine!

Imagine if he stands!

He would go through the roof!"

THE STATUE OF ZEUS AT OLYMPIA

Date built: 435 BC

Location: Greece

How long to build: 8–12 years

What happened: Earthquake

LOST ARTIFACT

Some say Phidias asked for a sign from Zeus. He wanted the god to be happy. Soon after, lightning struck the temple. It did no harm. A good sign.

His right hand held Nike.

The goddess of victory.

His left hand held a wand.

A *scepter*.

An eagle sat on top.

It was majestic.

A famous artist built the statue.

His name was Phidias.

It began with a wood frame.

On it sat Zeus.

He was carved from ivory.

And draped in gold.

This method is called

chryselephantine.

It showed much wealth.

And took years to build.

But this was for Zeus.

The king of all gods.

So it had to be the best.

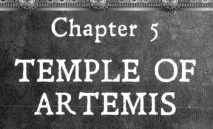

Chapter 5

TEMPLE OF ARTEMIS

The Greeks had many gods.

One was Artemis.

The goddess of the hunt.

People loved her.

They built her a *shrine*.

It was in Ephesus.

TEMPLE OF ARTEMIS

Date built: 550 BC

Location: Modern-day Turkey

How long to build: 120 years

What happened: Burned down

25

Not just any shrine.

This one was grand.

It was famous for its size.

And *columns*.

There were 127 of them.

Each was 60 feet tall.

And made of marble.

Inside the temple was the statue.

It was a work of art.

Made of gold.

Ebony.

And black stone.

All were very costly.

BEFORE DAMAGE

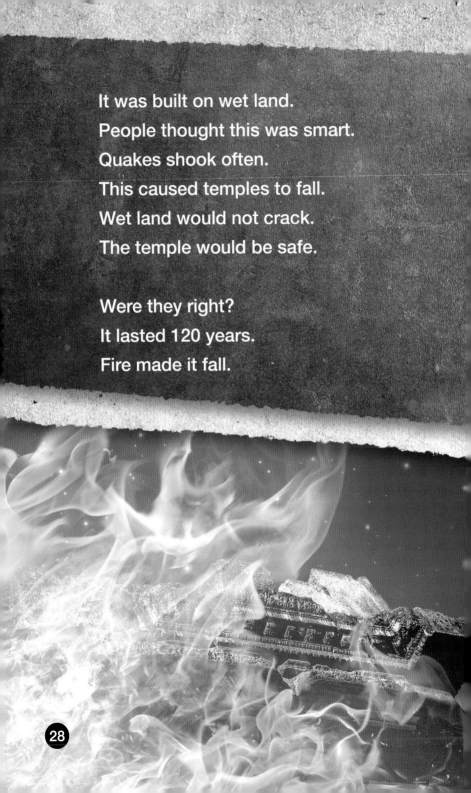

It was built on wet land.

People thought this was smart.

Quakes shook often.

This caused temples to fall.

Wet land would not crack.

The temple would be safe.

Were they right?

It lasted 120 years.

Fire made it fall.

A madman did it.

Arson.

People were angry.

They wanted a new temple.

It had to be big.

It had to shine.

They rebuilt it.

Three times.

One column stands today.

It reminds us of what was.

It proves the temple was real.

LOST ARTIFACT

The site where the temple once stood is now a swamp.

Chapter 6

THE HANGING GARDENS OF BABYLON

This story might be hard to believe.

But it is one of the most famous.

It goes back 2,000 years.

A king ruled in a desert.

A desert between two rivers.

The king married.

His queen came from far away.

She missed her home.

She missed the green land.

She missed the trees.

The king wanted to make her happy.

He had a garden built for her.

The lushest garden of all.

Flowers.

Trees.

A gift to his queen.

To remind her of home.

THE HANGING GARDENS OF BABYLON

Date built: 600 BC

Location: Modern-day Iraq

How long to build: Unknown

What happened: Earthquake

LOST ARTIFACT

Keeping the gardens green would have taken a lot of water. Some say 8,200 gallons of water each day.

It was said that the plants were on the roofs.
The leaves may have hung down.
Flowers too.
But did the plants hang at all?
There is no proof.

Is this story a legend?
Or is it real?
There is no *evidence* of this wonder.
It could just be a story.
Some say the garden was vast.
Over 300 feet high.
56 miles long.
Large.
Lush.
How could that be?
There is little water in the desert.
Could it have been a *mirage*?

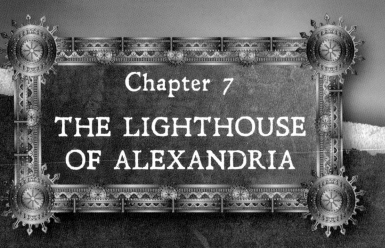

Chapter 7

THE LIGHTHOUSE OF ALEXANDRIA

There was another wonder in Egypt.

It was a tower.

It stood on a *delta*.

Near the Nile River.

There was a leader.

Alexander the Great.

He founded a city in his name.

He wanted a place near the Nile.

An island.

But not just any island.

One connected to the mainland.

THE LIGHTHOUSE OF ALEXANDRIA

Date built: 280 BC

Location: Egypt

How long to build: 12–20 years

What happened: Earthquake

Alexander died of a fever.
He was only 32 years old.
The tower was made in his name.
It was built in three stages.
The bottom was square.
The middle had eight sides.
The top was shaped like a barrel.
The tower was very tall.
It stood over 380 feet.

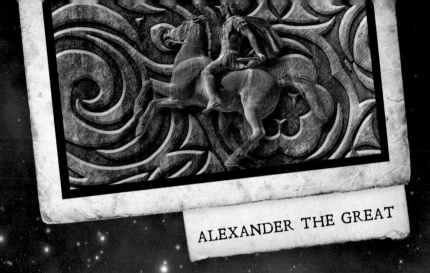

ALEXANDER THE GREAT

LOST ARTIFACT

In 1994, French archaeologists discovered some remains of the lighthouse on the floor of Alexandria's Eastern Harbor.

At the *apex* was a mirror.

It would reflect the sun.

This helped ships see where to go.

At night there was no sun.

So the top held a flame.

It could be seen for miles.

This was the first lighthouse.

Chapter 8

THE COLOSSUS AT RHODES

Rhodes was a busy city.

It was on an island.

Its people were proud.

They had won a war.

They beat back invaders.

Now they were free.

They wanted to thank the gods.

So they made a shrine.

It took many years.

The enemy fled after the war.

They left fast.

They dropped their weapons.

Left their machines.

The people used these things.

Metal was melted.

Iron and bronze.

These metals made the statue.

How do we know?

From ancient stories.

THE COLOSSUS AT RHODES

Date built: 292–280 BC

Location: Greece

How long to build: 12 years

What happened: Earthquake

The statue was of Helios.

The god of the sun.

It was 100 feet tall.

The tallest statue of the time.

It could be seen from far away.

But it did not last long.

It stood less than fifty years.

A quake struck.

The statue cracked.

Then it fell.

It lay like that for a long time.

People still came to visit.

They wanted to see the sun god.

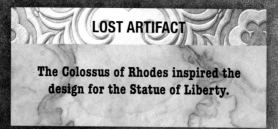

LOST ARTIFACT

The Colossus of Rhodes inspired the design for the Statue of Liberty.

Chapter 9

MAUSOLEUM OF HALICARNASSUS

Mausolus was a *satrap*.

A leader.

He wanted to build a new city.

To keep his people safe.

He wanted it to be grand.

He chose the spot.

Near the sea.

His men prepared the area.

But the *harbor* was too open.

The enemy could get in.

It was too easy.

The leader wanted it to be safe.

So he had mounds built.

The mounds held back waves.

They also kept the entrance small.

His ships could block and protect.

The harbor was finished.

The city was next.

Streets were paved.

Houses and shops were built.

The hard work paid off.

The city was safe.

The people were happy.

MAUSOLEUM OF HALICARNASSUS

Date built: 351 BC

Location: Modern-day Turkey

How long to build: Unknown

What happened: Earthquake

The leader died.

His wife wanted a tomb built.

She chose white marble for the walls.

She filled it with art.

She wanted a statue.

One that looked like her husband.

On a cart pulled by horses.

Flying off into the sky.

This was a big job.

It took many years.

She died before it was done.

She was buried with her husband.

Artists kept working.

They made a statue of her.

She also sat in the cart.

They could fly off into the sky together.

LOST ARTIFACT

The word "mausoleum" comes from the tomb of Mausolus.

Chapter 10

OTHER WONDERS?

People study the past.

They find clues.

Buried objects.

Proof of buildings.

Cities.

Bones.

The clues tell a story.

They tell us about history.

But there are also stories.

Ancient tales.

These also tell us about the past.

Some stories are about real things.

They give us clues.

Some are myths.

They are made up.

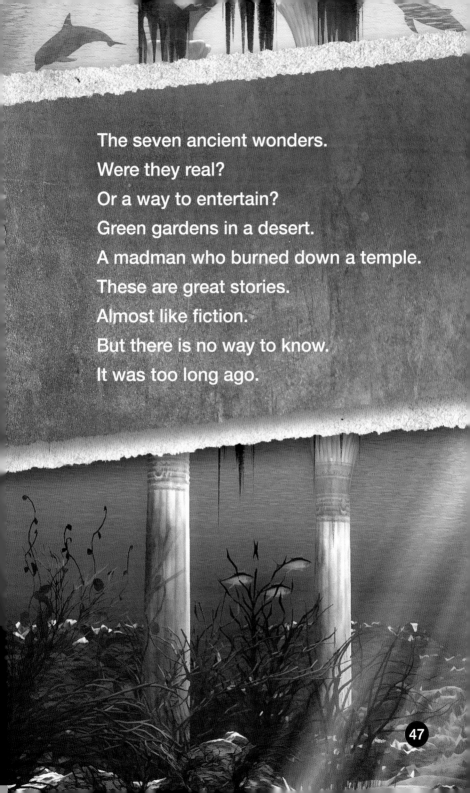

The seven ancient wonders.

Were they real?

Or a way to entertain?

Green gardens in a desert.

A madman who burned down a temple.

These are great stories.

Almost like fiction.

But there is no way to know.

It was too long ago.

One thing is for sure.

People still talk about these wonders.

There were seven.

So people stick with that number.

They make new lists.

The seven natural wonders.

The seven wonders of today.

Huge waterfalls.

Deep, vast canyons.

Large coral reefs.

A Great Wall.

People travel far to see them.

You might see them one day.

Then it will be your turn.

You can be the storyteller.

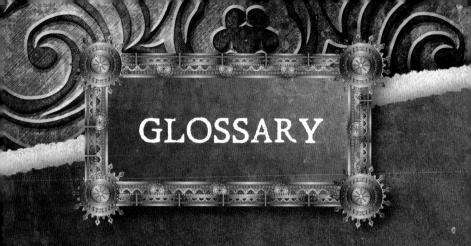

GLOSSARY

adorn: decorate

ancient: very old

apex: the very top

arson: starting a fire illegally

artifacts: objects from the past made by humans

chryselephantine: covered with gold and ivory

column: a tall round structure that helps hold up a building

delta: a piece of land that forms at the mouth of a river

entertain: make people laugh and feel happy

evidence: proof something is real

harbor: a place near the coast where ships can dock and be out of rough water

limestone: a hard white rock

mirage: something that looks real from a distance but is not

pharaoh: the top leader in ancient Egypt

pyramid: a structure with a square or triangular base and sloping slides that meet at a point at the top

satrap: a leader

scepter: a decorated pole that kings and queens hold

shrine: a place to honor a god

statue: a large piece of art made to look like a person or animal

temple: a place for people to worship a god

TAKE A LOOK INSIDE

Witchcraft

They knew about plants.
They made medicine.
A drink for a fever.
A lotion for a burn.
A bandage for a sprain.

People trusted them.
They knew everyone.
They kept secrets.
Some did not like this.
The Roman Catholic Church.
The Church wanted people's trust.
And *loyalty*.
They said witches were bad.
People got scared.
Witches were jailed.
Many were killed.
So they hid.
Worked in secret.

FEVER

There were trials.
They started in Europe.
Then they came to America.
To *colonial* Hartford. Then Salem.
There were laws.
No witches. No magic.
It was a crime.

There is still fear today.
Most witches stay hidden.
They keep quiet. Work alone.
They may trust other witches.
And form a group.
They call it a *coven*.

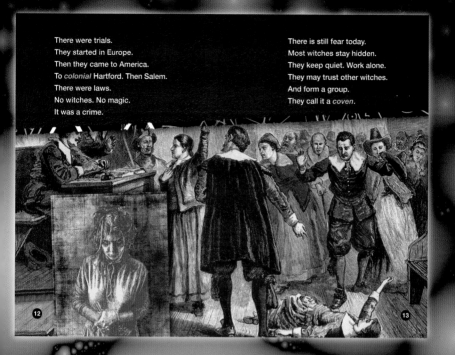

Palm reading is older.
It began in ancient India.
Around 500 BC.
Palms have lines.
There are three main ones.
Heart. Or feelings.
Head. Or the mind.
Life. Or happiness.

The right hand is the future.
And the outer self.
The left hand is the past.
And the inner self.

red rhino books®

NONFICTION

9781680210293

9781680210286

9781680210309

9781680210330

9781680210361

9781680210323

9781680210316

9781680210538

9781680210347

9781680210354

9781680210491

9781680210521

9781680210378

9781680210484

MORE
TITLES
COMING
SOON